Animals Close Up

DOGS CLOSE UP

By Seth Lynch

Gareth Stevens
PUBLISHING

Please visit our website, www.garethstevens.com. For a free color catalog of all our high-quality books, call toll free 1-800-542-2595 or fax 1-877-542-2596.

Library of Congress Cataloging-in-Publication Data
Names: Lynch, Seth, author.
Title: Dogs close up/ Seth Lynch.
Description: New York : Gareth Stevens Publishing, [2023] | Series: Animals close up | Includes index.
Identifiers: LCCN 2021040653 (print) | LCCN 2021040654 (ebook) | ISBN 9781538281246 (set) | ISBN 9781538281253 (library binding) | ISBN 9781538281239 (paperback) | ISBN 9781538281260 (ebook)
Subjects: LCSH: Dogs–Juvenile literature.
Classification: LCC SF426.5 .L97 2023 (print) | LCC SF426.5 (ebook) | DDC 636.7–dc23
LC record available at https://lccn.loc.gov/2021040653
LC ebook record available at https://lccn.loc.gov/2021040654

First Edition

Published in 2023 by
Gareth Stevens Publishing
29 East 21st Street
New York, NY 10010

Editor: Kristen Nelson
Designer: Rachel Rising

Photo credits: Cover, p. 1 Prystai/Shutterstock.com; p. 5 Irina Kozorog/Shutterstock.com; p. 7 Dmetsov Alexey/Shutterstock.com; pp. 9, 24 alexei_tm/Shutterstock.com; p. 11 Bonita R. Cheshier/Shutterstock.com; pp. 13, 24 Liudmila Bohush/Shutterstock.com; p. 15 Grisha Bruev/Shutterstock.com; p. 17 TMArt/Shutterstock.com; p. 19 Weerameth Weerachotewong/Shutterstock.com; pp. 21, 24 Anna Hoychuk/Shutterstock.com; p. 23 Di Studio/Shutterstock.com.

Printed in the United States of America

CPSIA compliance information: Batch #CSGS23: For further information contact Gareth Stevens, New York, New York at 1-800-542-2595.

Contents

Dogs are a popular pet. There are more than 400 kinds!

They can have long or short noses.
They have a great sense of smell.

Dogs have big teeth.
Adults have 42.

Some dogs' ears
are floppy.
Some point up.
Great Danes' ears
point up.

Dogs have fur.
This is their coat.

Some have a long coat.

Pointers have a short coat.

Many dogs lose some of their coat. This is shedding.

Dogs have four legs. Their feet are paws. They have four main toes.

Most dogs have a tail.
It may be long or short!

Words to Know

coat

paw

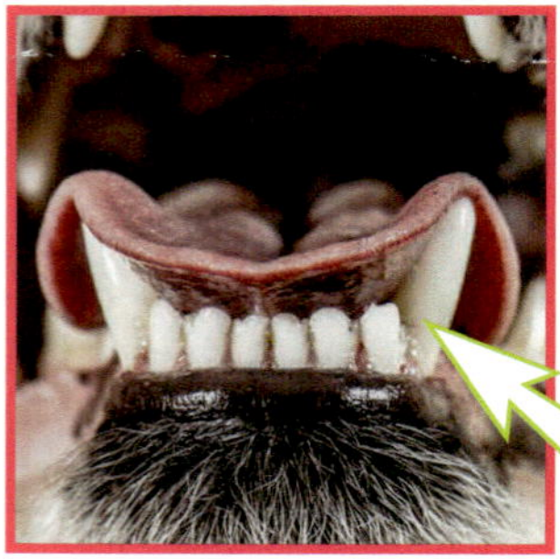

teeth

Index